This book is dedicated to our family and friends, including the current and future Pliable athletes who continue to help increase the popularity of women's sports, and make the world a better place.

We're grateful you've decided to share this book with a child in your life, because we believe you, can make a difference in the life of a child.

Thank you,

Greg and Kelsey

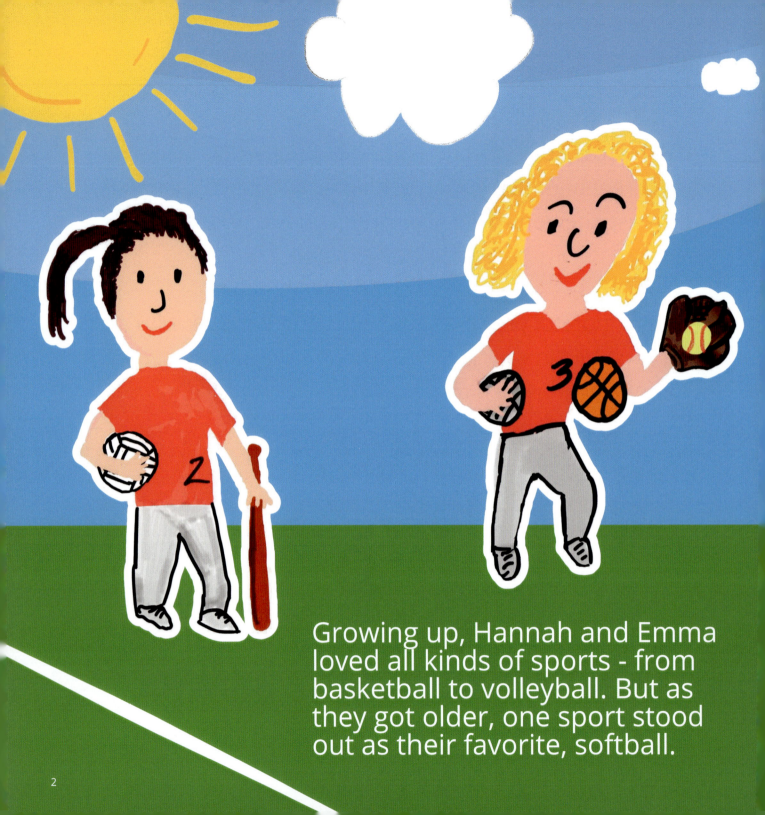

Growing up, Hannah and Emma loved all kinds of sports - from basketball to volleyball. But as they got older, one sport stood out as their favorite, softball.

When Hannah and Emma were younger, there weren't that many softball teams, so sometimes they had to play with the boys.

One thing they enjoyed about softball was being part of a team. They got to hang out with their friends, practice after school, and catch up on girl talk.

Both Hannah and Emma had the same dream, to play college softball. To play college softball, you have to be *really* good. You also have to get good grades and be involved in your community.

Hannah and Emma practiced softball a lot with their parents and coaches, so they could get better every day.

Emma grew up in the small town of Santa Claus, Indiana, where she volunteered at the local hospital, played for her high school team, and was an All-Star.

Hannah grew up in Saint Joseph, Illinois, where softball wasn't as popular as it is today. Hannah loved softball because she was *really* fast. Like Emma, she was an All-Star on her high school team, but that's not the only thing they had in common.

Hannah and Emma ended up applying to the exact same college, for the exact same reason; they wanted to play softball, but most importantly they wanted to help kids who have cancer. Cancer is a disease that impacts a person's health for a long period of time.

Hannah lost both of her grandfathers because of cancer. She was really close to her grandparents who lived next door. Her grandfather was one of her biggest fans, he would come to all her games. He was also the person who always encouraged her to smile.

Emma's family has also been deeply affected by cancer. When she feels sad, she relies on her faith and her memories with the people who have had cancer, including her favorite teacher who passed away.

Emma and Hannah met for the first time when they arrived at college. They were roommates and would spend a lot of time together. They became the best of friends. They played softball together; they studied together, they were inseparable.

Hannah and Emma would always set goals for themselves, just like they did when they were little kids and wanted to be college softball players.

When they were in college, they decided that one of their life goals was going to be to help children who have cancer.

One day, Hannah and Emma decided they would combine their passion for softball with their career goal by using their sport to raise money for childhood cancer research. They decided to paint their softball cleats so everyone would know that finding a cure for cancer was **very** important to them.

Every time Emma and Hannah put on their cleats they would think about their family and friends who have been impacted by cancer. But it wasn't just their family and friends who started to notice. Their teammates and opponents saw their cleats and thought, what a cool idea!

Emma and Hannah's idea was so popular that TV stations, newspapers, magazines, and podcasters started to tell the story about why they painted their cleats. Other softball players started doing it, too.

The cleats were very special to Hannah and Emma because they wore them *a lot*. At the end of the season, instead of keeping them for themselves, they decided to sell them online.

The reason they decided to sell their cleats was to raise money for childhood cancer research.

Hannah and Emma's decision to sell their cleats led to more opportunities to extend their group of friends and supporters. They even got invited to a National Childhood Cancer Awareness Walk.

Hannah and Emma were so excited to be able to invite all their friends and family to participate in the walk; everyone raised money and formed a huge team called Team #CURECANCER.

At the fundraising walk, Hannah and Emma were invited on stage to talk about what they had done with their cleats. When they added up the total from the cleats they sold and the money their team donated, they raised **$4,500** for childhood cancer research!

After the walk, they met even more people, including children with childhood cancer. Hannah and Emma became heroes to the children and their families because of what they did with their magic cleats.

During their final college season together, Hannah and Emma wore cleats designed by children with illnesses. After their last game, they also decided to sell a gold-colored glove to raise more money for cancer research.

In a sport measured by wins and losses, Hannah and Emma had learned a valuable lesson, that some of the **greatest** victories in life, don't always happen on a softball field.

Not the end.

This is where a *typical* children's book ends, but what makes this book unique is that it is a true and ongoing story.

On April 8, 2023, Emma Eubank (left) and Hannah Dukeman (right) became the first college athletes in the country to use their name, image and likeness (NIL) to wear #CURECANCER cleats and auction them off for charity.

Their donation of $4,500 to the St. Jude Children's Research Hospital has directly inspired other athletes who heard about their story. Since then, more Pliable athletes continue to use their name, image and likeness to support causes and community projects that are important to them. By reading this book, you are now part of Hannah and Emma's story and can help continue to raise awareness and funds for childhood cancer research. You already have helped, because a portion of the proceeds from this book will benefit cancer research and #MissionE50.

The following pages are optional for young children. The "bonus" pages are included to share more details about Hannah and Emma's story and inspire every person who reads this book.

Hannah Dukeman is from Saint Joseph, Illinois and went to Ball State University as a double major in pre-med preparation and biology with a minor in chemistry and Spanish. She graduated in May of 2024 with a Bachelor of Science degree and a 3.83 GPA. Her career goal is to work with families and children who have been impacted by cancer.

Hannah was a center fielder and pinch runner for the Cardinals. To this day, she still enjoys playing softball and teaching the game to the next generation.

In 2024, Hannah and Emma were the recipients of the Heart of the Cardinal Award at the 2024 Chirpies.

Learn more about Hannah using the QR code below.

Emma Eubank is from Santa Claus, Indiana and went to Ball State University to get her degree pre-medical preparation (double major), advanced biotechnology certificate with a minor in chemistry. She was the Head Lab Technician at Ball State, where she spent hundreds of hours in the lab to find the cure for cancer. She graduated in May of 2024 with a Bachelor of Science degree and a 3.79 GPA.

Emma was a left-handed pitcher and had a career ERA of 5.32. She won the last game she ever pitched.

In 2024, Emma was the only Ball State athlete nominated for the NCAA Postgraduate Scholarship which recognizes the top athletes in the country for outstanding records in academics, leadership, and service.

After graduation, she was accepted by Vanderbilt University to pursue a six-year program to get her PhD in cancer research. Emma's career goal is to scientifically find a cure for childhood cancer.

Learn more about Emma by using the QR code below.

Hannah and Emma designed their own cleats, which were then customized and painted by Stadium Custom Kicks. In their final season, they also partnered with Souls 2 Hope, a nonprofit organization that provides encouragement, support and hope for children fighting critical health battles through advocacy and collaboration with the power of sports.

Hannah and Emma have been featured in several media stories about their magic cleats. They were even featured on the cover of *Money Talks* magazine as the 2023 Advocates of the Year.

To commemorate their careers, they signed a NIL partnership with the Wylde Glove company to create a gold glove, which represents the color of childhood cancer with the hashtag #CURECANCER embroidered on the glove. They decided to auction off the glove to raise more awareness and funds for childhood cancer research.

Hannah and Emma's story doesn't just stop there. They are both Pliable athletes and have had their story told to hundreds of athletes. Pliable is a marketing company and NIL agency that represents high school, college, and professional athletes from across the country.

Every Pliable athlete is told Hannah and Emma's story.
As a result, their story has inspired many athletes to use their name, image and likeness for charitable and community endeavors.

The following pages include inspirational stories about more Pliable athletes.

Inspired #PliableAthletes

Kaylyn Bourque (left) and Alyssa Bourque (right), sisters from Benton, Maine, made history by signing the first official NIL partnership in Maine when they used their name, image and likeness to donate $5,000 to the Waterville Humane Society. Kaylyn and Alyssa created a public service announcement and made posts on social media.

Inspired #PliableAthlete

Sadie Armstrong (left), a softball player from Portland, Maine, created a one-of-a-kind scholarship program to help young softball players afford to play travel softball and get recruited by college coaches.

Inspired #PliableAthlete

Natalie Beaudoin, a basketball player from Lewiston, Maine, designed T-shirts following the mass shooting in Lewiston on October 25, 2023. The shirts read "We are Lew1ston" and raised more than $1,000 to support the victims and the families following the tragedy in her home state.

Inspired #PliableAthlete

Alana LaCourse (right) is a dancer and ski racer from East Boothbay, Maine. At age 15, Alana created GIVE O.N.E., a nonprofit that helps more young children compete in ski racing by providing new and used ski equipment.

Inspired #PliableAthlete

Logan Hale (left), a golfer from Erie, Colorado, established Putting for Puppies, a youth golf clinic to raise awareness and funds for Lifeline Puppy Rescue, an animal shelter in her home state that supports the well-being of animals.

Inspired #PliableAthletes

Ella Boerger, Maddie Brown, JuliAnna and Jenessa Gazdik and Cara Sajevic (left to right), all Division 1 women's ice hockey players, volunteered at the Hendrickson Foundation's National Hockey Festival in Blaine, Minnesota. The foundation's mission is to grow the game of hockey by making it accessible to all people, despite any challenges they may be living with and creating a stronger and more inclusive State of Hockey.

Inspired #PliableAthlete

Alyssa Bourque (right), a track and field athlete from Benton, Maine, became the first community ambassador in the country for Aroma Joe's. Her networking connection to meet Crystal Brown (left) from Aroma Joe's was named the 2023 Pliable Connection of the Year. As a result of her community work, and other Pliable athletes, Aroma Joe's Development Office continues to expand its community ambassador program which has become one of the most impactful name, image and likeness programs in the country.

Inspired #PliableAthlete

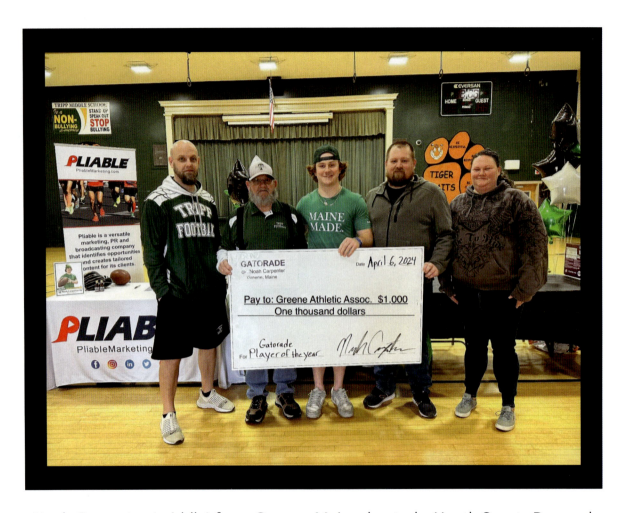

Noah Carpenter (middle) from Greene, Maine, hosted a Youth Sports Day and donated $1,000 to the Greene Athletic Association as part of a food drive and fundraiser for the Turner Community Food Pantry. By the end of the event, Carpenter collected all types of food and raised more than $370.

Inspired #PliableAthlete

Lauren Knight, a field hockey player from Orleans, Massachusetts, signed a NIL partnership with the Northeast Sports Card Expo to raise money for Tommy's Place, a dream vacation home for kids fighting cancer and their families. The home is located in Falmouth, Massachusetts on Cape Cod.

Inspired #PliableAthlete

Maddie Niles, a field hockey player from Benton, Maine, has raised funds for the Ronald McDonald House, Family Violence Project and the Travis Mills Foundation. In high school, she signed a NIL partnership with Hilltop Boilers Maple Syrup which was the first of its kind in the country. Maddie is also a community ambassador for Aroma Joe's Development Office of Maine and New Hampshire.

Inspired #PliableAthlete

Amber Bretton (middle), a softball player from Gorham, Maine, used her name, image and likeness at the Northeast Sports Card Expo to raise money for the One Lewiston Resiliency Fund. The organization supports the city of Lewiston following the tragic mass shooting in her home state in 2023. Amber is also a community ambassador for Aroma Joe's Development Office and partnered with the company to help sell "STRONGER TOGETHER" T-shirts to raise additional funds for organizations and nonprofits.

Inspired #PliableAthlete

Kelsey Glynn, a dancer from Augusta, Maine, has raised more than $1,000 for the Maine Children's Home in Waterville. Year-round, Kelsey spends much of her free time helping the organization prepare for their annual Christmas Program, which provides new clothes, winter essentials, toys, books, and games to Maine children and families who are facing financial hardship. She also helped write and illustrate this book to share the legacy of two of her role models, Hannah and Emma.

To be continued...

While many athletes will make money using their name, image and likeness, Pliable athletes are carefully selected because of their strong personal values and character. Each athlete is educated and empowered for success during and after their playing career.

To date, Pliable athletes in this book and others have raised more than $20,000 for nonprofits and community events.

If your child is looking for a positive role model and an athlete to look up to, please encourage them to check out the growing list of Pliable athletes at PliableMarketing.com/pliable-athletes or use the QR code below.

To see more inspirational stories and learn about Pliable athletes, you can search #pliableathlete on social media.
You might even find an athlete near you!

Follow @PliableMktg on social media to get the latest news and stories about the team of Pliable athletes.

We appreciate your support!

About the Authors

Greg Glynn is the Founder & CEO of Pliable, a marketing, PR and broadcasting company. Greg develops personal relationships with high school, college, and professional athletes to help them build their athlete brand, including securing name, image and likeness opportunities.

Greg is a registered athlete agent in many states and is the creator of #MissionE50, an initiative to increase the popularity of women's sports. As part of #MissionE50, Greg helped Hannah and Emma to bring the idea for their #CURECANCER cleats to life.

Kelsey Glynn is the daughter of Greg and Cindy Glynn. Kelsey is a Pliable athlete, just like Hannah and Emma. She was heavily involved in the writing of the book to inspire the next generation of young girls to become positive role models. Kelsey is well-known for her efforts to raise awareness and funds for the Maine Children's Home in Waterville, Maine.

During the COVID-19 pandemic, Kelsey became one of the youngest athletes to raise funds and complete the 180-mile Trek Across Maine bike ride to benefit the American Lung Association.

About #MISSIONE50

#MissionE50 is an initiative created by Pliable's Founder & CEO, Greg Glynn. The purpose of #MissionE50 is to increase the popularity of women's sports. By reading this book, Greg, Kelsey and the other Pliable athletes believe it will inspire young athletes, especially young girls to set big goals and go after their dreams.

Proceeds from this book will benefit #MissionE50 and fundraising efforts for cancer research. Thank you for purchasing this book and supporting Pliable athletes and our mission. To learn more, search #MissionE50 on social media, visit PliableMarketing.com/e50 or scan the QR code.